PARSONS BREAD BOOK

A celebration of the art of baking bread
and the great bakers of New York City
by students at Parsons School of Design,
who made this book:
David Blumenthal, Vicky Coleman, Chris Grana,
Sherry Gutberlet, Peter Mattes, Ed Mazzola, Fran Rappaport,
Dot Scott, Carolyn Sievers, Pat Valle, Bonnie Weber,
and Cipe Pineles Burtin, faculty.

Harper & Row, Publishers
New York, Evanston, San Francisco, London

Dedicated to all who love bread

ISBN 0-06-013282-5
Library of Congress Catalog
Card Number 73-14280

ingredients

bread

This book evolved from a project in publication design, assigned by internationally-known art-director/faculty member Cipe Pineles Burtin to her class in our department of Communication Design. Each spring term Ms. Burtin's class has had the responsibility of producing a yearbook for the college. This year it was their decision that the book should deal with material that was representative of student interests and values without being strictly autobiographical.

Bread (the title under which this book was originally published) was the result. There is nothing except political activism that better demonstrates the desire of today's young people to change the "plastic" world of galloping consumerism than their revival of the traditional crafts. The baking of bread has been one of the most popular. This, coupled with the knowledge that there is still a viable baking tradition in New York and in many other cities and towns, led the students to explore this subject as an expression of their concern for a more honest world. Then too, a good loaf of bread is almost a work of art—there is nothing that quite compares with the experience of seeing, touching, smelling, and finally tasting a freshly baked loaf. And if you have baked it yourself, these satisfactions are increased manyfold.

So the students who wrote, designed, photographed, illustrated, and produced this book during a hectic three months in the spring of 1973 participated in an experience that was creative on many levels. As this edition of *Parsons Bread Book* goes to press, most of them are graduates working as designers and art directors in the New York publishing and advertising industries.

It is gratifying to all of us at Parsons to know that this book, first published in a very limited student edition and representing three aroma-filled months of all-night baking, photographing, writing, designing, and tasting, will now reach a wider audience.

David C. Levy
Dean, Parsons School of Design

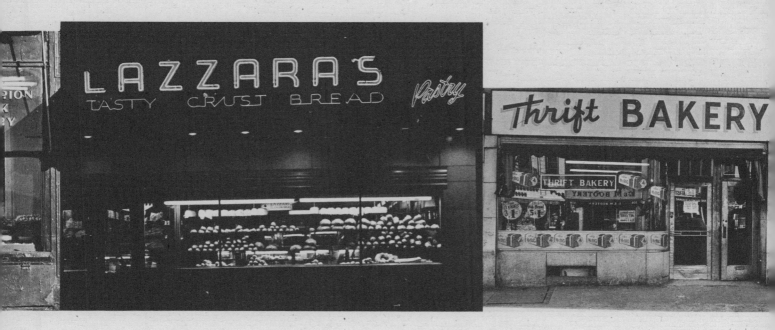

baking at Zito's is a family tradition, but will it all end when Julius Zito and his brother retire?

Zito's Bakery
259 Bleecker Street
New York, New York
212/WA 9-6139

On Wednesday, April 4, 1973, Zito's Bakery was packed with customers congratulating bakery owners Frances, Julius, and Charlie Zito on their recent appearance in a *New York Magazine* article. The customers greeted the owners by their first names; warm wishes, jokes, and tips about how to remain in the limelight were exchanged. The atmosphere was so friendly and warm that smiling was contagious. The Zito family has been baking at their present location for forty-eight years, and Julius Zito was born in the small apartment behind the store.

The Zitos believe that bread is good only when it is made naturally. The two brick ovens in the basement were built about one hundred years ago and are fueled with coal since the Zitos feel gas and oil kill the taste of bread. Baking is done by hand. Three work shifts prepare the dough for the finished loaves virtually around the clock.

A long-time customer who describes himself as a world traveler said that Zito's bread is simply the best he has ever tasted. He credits its fabulous flavor to the ovens that are used, where the bread is placed directly on top of the hot bricks.

Julius Zito feels that since his son is in medical school and his daughter is a teacher, his business is in danger of closing when he and his brother retire. He also unhappily foresees totally automated bakeries in the future if young people do not become involved in local-home bakeries where the baking process is done manually, and the dough is lovingly kneaded by hand.

Top Row: One baker weighs the dough for the other baker to knead it into the desired shape.
Whole wheat loaves being placed in the hearth ovens on a long wooden peel.

The shop window is filled with an assortment of Zito's finished breads.
Bottom Row: Whole wheat loaves taken from the oven.

9

"the best bagels in Brooklyn"

Golden Bakery
533 Kings Highway
Brooklyn, New York
212/DE 9-9834

"The best bagels in Brooklyn" is a tribute worthy of note, and the bakers at Louis Schilowitz's Golden Bakery work constantly to keep their bagels great.

A bagel, defined by the dictionary as a "hard, glazed donut-shaped roll," comes in seven varieties at the Golden Bakery. The plain, onion, garlic, sesame, poppy seed, salted, and pumpernickel rings are baked daily until 6 PM. One hundred and twenty-five dozen bagels are made every day and the store is open from 8 AM to 10 PM seven days a week.

At the Golden Bakery, bakers first prepare the dough, then shape and set it into wooden boxes that have been sprinkled with corn meal to prevent sticking. The dough is then left to rise. After two hours, it is placed in a retarder.

When it is finally time to bake the bagels, they are first placed in boiling water for two minutes to make them shine. Next, they are thrown onto a slide. Each baker then takes six bagels from the slide and puts them on a long, rectangular board where they are seasoned. At last, they are placed in the oven.

BIALYS   GARLIC   SESAME   ONION

There are three steps for baking bagels 1) Shaping and forming the bagels; 2) Boiling them for 2 minutes; 3) Just before entering oven, bagels are seasoned with poppy seeds, sesame seeds, garlic, or salt.

young bakers must learn the baking process
from wheat to customer

Seventy-two years ago, in the back of another store, the Lazzara family opened a bakery which made deliveries in a horse-drawn wagon. As their reputation and business grew, differ-ent members of the family were brought in to distribute advertising leaflets and work in the bakery.

The family tradition was vital, and even today, despite modern machinery and baking methods, young bakers must learn every step of the business—from the wheat to the customer. The Lazzara Bakery guards its famous recipes as though they were gold. The bakery produces

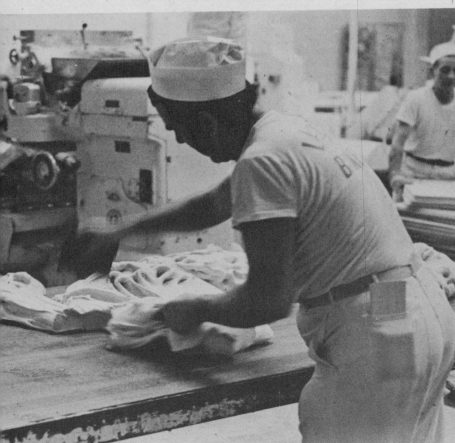

one hundred and seventy-four different kinds of bread, and work continues seven days a week, twenty-four hours a day. Lazzara Bakery is the largest of its kind in the entire world. There are three plants where the actual baking is done, and Lazzara Bread is sold in New York, New Jersey, Pennsylvania, Connecticut and Maryland. The bakery also supplies schools in New York, and army, navy, and air force and hospitals.

Lazzara Products
45 Park Street
Paterson, New Jersey
201/742-2424

a new life style for Harry Appel

In 1964, Harry Appel bought the Patisserie Parisienne, now the Paris Pastry Shop, from Charles Burel. As the former general sales manager of a metal company, Mr. Appel must have seemed an unlikely candidate for a baker. Despite this, and without any formal training, he invested his life savings and took the plunge.

That was nine years ago, and today, family and staff efforts have paid off. Paris Bakery proucts are sold to caterers, count clubs, Bloomingdale's, cheese shops, and the Jugtown Mountain Smokehouse chain throug out New Jersey and New York Bread baking, a small percent the Shop's business, is done by traditional French standards. Mr. Appel's excellent croissant

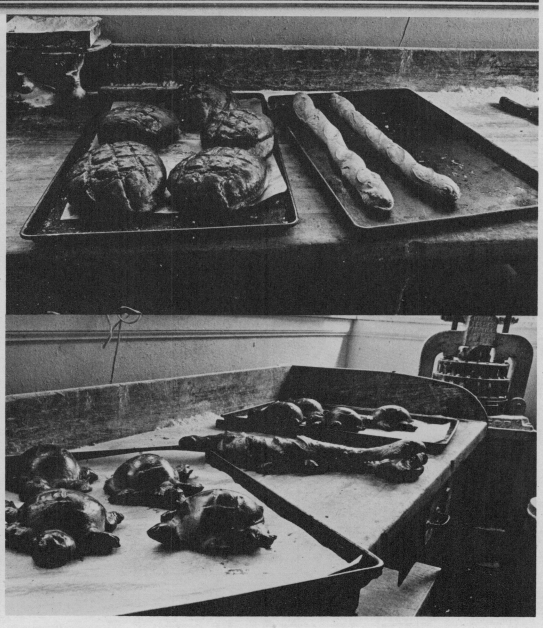

have even been served to the visiting Duke and Duchess of Windsor and the presidential family in the White House.

Realizing that a small bakery couldn't compete with larger firms by simply selling plain loaves, Harry Appel called upon other resources to make his breads more distinctive. His interest in painting transformed loaves of bread into alligators, turtles, rabbits, wreaths and snakes. His sourdough breads (long or round) don't try to copy the famous San Francisco sourdough. Appel's special sourdough recipe accents and complements the taste of cheese. The aroma of sourdough can be overwhelming, but as with good wine, taste improves with age. Meeting Harry Appel in his shop amidst its heady baking smells, a visitor is struck by the gentleness of this sensitive and skilled man whose work has been commended in the *Ridgewood News*, *The New York Times*, and *The Sunday News*.

With more business than his hands can handle, Harry Appel says "I like to think of our product as a comparison between a fine oil painting and a print of the same."

Paris Pastry Shop
171 East Ridgewood Avenue
Ridgewood, New Jersey
201/445-8880

our investigation of Orwasher's began with a good look at their 1916 hearth ovens.

A. Orwasher, Inc.
308 East 78 Street
New York, New York
212/BU 8-6569

Nostalgia and a sense of "old world" charm pervade the Orwasher Bakery on east 78th Street, New York City. Run by A. Orwasher and his sister, Sarah Rubin, the bakery offers its customers many different kinds of bread, baked in the same 1916 hearth oven first used by Orwasher's father.

The bakery sells bread for every type of taste. Rye bread, corn, potato, and whole wheat bread, challah, and raisin pumpernickel are all made without additives or preservatives and are sold by weight.

The bakery itself maintains the simple, gentle quality of a turn-of-the-century store. Bread that is ready to be sold is stacked on shelves and displayed in counter baskets. The bakery walls are white with segments of wood paneling, reminiscent of a wood-frame house. The courtesy and warm welcome each customer receives add the final perfect touch.

Mr. Orwasher's bread can be bought in many of the small food stores in the neighborhood, as well as at the bakery itself.

Top: The dough is rolled.
Next it is kneaded and shaped.
Some bread is baked in small
baking dishes.
Finally it is ready to be sold.

23

at Toufayan baking is a family affair

Toufayan Bakery
9255 Kennedy Blvd.
North Bergen, New Jersey
201/861-4131

The Toufayan Bakery is owned and operated by the Toufayan family. Arthur Toufayan, the head of the family, has been baking bread for forty-seven years.

Mr. Toufayan was born in Turkey, but fled to Egypt after the Massacre of 1915. It was there that he set up a bakery which he operated until 1962 when he came to America. After he and his family got settled, the Toufayan Bakery was re-established in West New York, using the same recipes and baking methods from the original bakery in Egypt.

This special bakery produces mostly Middle East "hollow bread" called Pita. The history of Pita Bread dates back about five thousand years. Its origin is Mesopotamia and its enduring success has been attributed to the purity of its ingredients.

The Toufayan Bakery also bakes a whole wheat Pita that is sold in various health food stores. The Pita breads are made without any preservatives. Meat pies, spinach pies, Armenian pizza, breadsticks, and an Armenian spread bread called Lavash are also made at the bakery with the help of Mrs. Toufayan, Sr.

Baking at Toufayan Bakery is carried on six days a week, for eight to ten hours a day. The bakery employs eight people who can each perform any of the tasks required to bake the bread.

Top: Dough for Pita bread is flattened.
Pita dough is rolled into balls on a special metal sheet and transferred to storage trays. Pita dough is flattened again.

Bottom: From trays, dough is placed on baking sheet and put in oven.
Hollow pita dough rises to make Toufayan's distinctive bread.

secrecy is not the only ingredient in the baking of French bread at Interbaco.

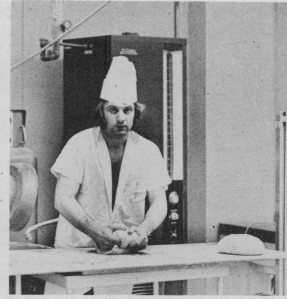

Top: ingredients for dough are
mixed.
Dough is divided and set aside
for about 10 minutes before
rolls are made.
Middle: Dough is shaped by
machine and placed on linen
cloth.
Bottom: bread and rolls are
removed from oven.

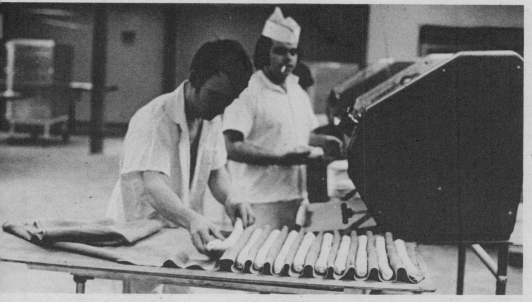

Interbaco
455 Eleventh Avenue
New York, New York
212/594-1813

Meeting the bakers at Interbaco
was about as easy as entering any
federally guarded nuclear weap-
ons testing plant. First, there
was the forbidding warehouse,
with a dimly lit second floor
and no welcome mat outside.
Then came the two strangers,
materializing from the darkness
to greet us, and the hurried
phone call in a nearby booth
when our identities had been
established. Next, the key to
the building was tossed out of
a second floor window as we
drew near the warehouse, and
finally, miraculously, we reached
the inside of the plant, where
bakers produce these famous
breads.

29

Top: Rolls set on board to rise.
Bottom: Cutting dough with
scissors to make Empire bread.

Dough is put on belt before
entering oven.

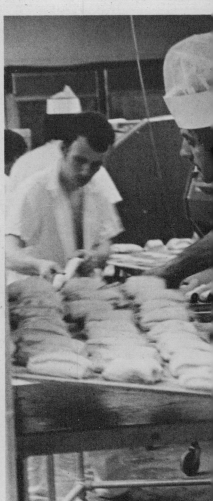

La Parisienne is removed from oven and placed in crates for delivery.

Removing Versailles from oven.

Christian Domerque is the manager of Interbaco which obtains its vital, sophisticated equipment from a French company called Pavailler.

Each day, Interbaco produces one thousand dozen rolls, one thousand Parisienne loaves, four hundred and fifty-two Empire breads, four hundred and sixty-four Versailles — and five hundred and eighty three Baguette loaves. All of these famous breads are baked from the same Interbaco dough mixture using flour, water, salt, and yeast.

Interbaco's reputation is outstanding and the bakery bakes the bread served in restaurants in New York. It also supplies American supermarket chains like Sloan's and D'Agostino's.

The Pavailler Company intends to use its New York Interbaco baking operation as a training school for future franchised French bakeries across the U.S. At present, classes for ten bakers at a time can be accommodated over a fifteen-day training period.

the neon window sign boldly proclaims "Mosha's Bakery."

Mosha's Bakery
170 Sythe Avenue
Brooklyn, New York
212/EV 7-7049

The inside of Mosha's Bakery is devoid of the counter, cash register, window displays and high glass cabinets that usually identify a bakery. In their place there is only the owner Sam Erde, a very content-looking man who sits behind a desk. On the walls behind him there are two telephones, various diplomas and awards, and a number of pictures that were painted by his grandchildren. In fact, the only thing that leads you to suspect

you are actually inside a baker is the bold neon window sign, "Mosha's Breads."

But Mosha's Bakery is one of t last of the old-time bakeries, where all the work is done by hand. And walking through to the back of the store, the bake itself is finally revealed.

At Mosha's Bakery there is very little machinery for baking. Three bakers, working under fluorescent lighting, keep watc over the bread dough which is naturally fermented and requir a twenty-four-hour check.

Beneath the street floor the bre are actually baked in brick ove They can weigh from two to

Sam Erde holds one of his unique breads.

Top Right: Bakers knead and mold bread dough.

wenty pounds, and the average
read weighs about five pounds.
Mr. Erde explained that the larg-
r loaves taste and smell better
because they take longer to bake
nd therefore more flavor and
roma are developed within the
oven.
Mosha's Bakery does a limited re-
ail business with New York
estaurants like Zum Zum's,
Charley O's, The Clip Joint at
he Statler Hilton and Improvi-
ation. It was started in 1890,
when Sam Erde's father and
randfather found an envelope
ontaining seventeen dollars on
he street, and decided to open
 bakery.

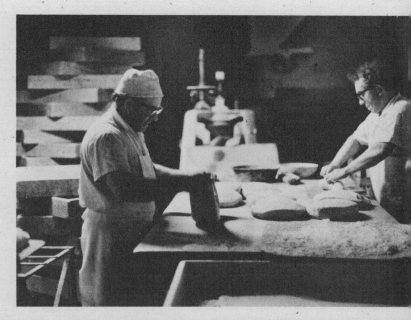

hard work and love lend their own kind of magic to breads baked by Magic Mommy

Hard work, experimentation, and love are the ingredients that make magic shapes at the bakery owned and operated by Robin and Kenneth Lee Karpe.

"Magic Mommy," the Karpes' unique bakery, started more than seven years ago when Robin Karpe began to bake cakes and cookies for her children and their friends. At the time, her enchanting creations earned her the name "Magic Mommy" and the bakery that subsequently developed on the family's Stony Hollow, New York farm, was called Magic Mommy too.

Robin Karpe's concern for nutritious as well as appetizing food soon led her to develop her own recipes for bread. These recipes were so successful that friends encouraged her to market the bread in local health food stores.

Once people tried Magic Mommy bread, a great demand for it grew. In order to handle the increasing numbers of orders, the Karpes built a special bakery extension off the back of their house. Some commercial equipment was also bought, but the basic ingredients and original recipes remained as they had been in Magic Mommy's own kitchen.

The commitment to good health is part of the Karpes' life style, and Magic Mommy bread is baked accordingly. No preservatives are added to the stone ground flour or to the final product. Whenever possible, the natural ingredients are grown on the Karpes' own farm. Carrots, dill and onions are grown here, and when in season Magic Mommy collects wild mushrooms in the local woods and shallots from the stream beds that meander through their farm. Goat's milk, considered finer than cow's milk, is produced by the family's own animals, and their chickens lay the eggs that are needed to bake the bread.

The people at Magic Mommy bake one thousand loaves a night, six nights a week. The bread is sold in many health food stores and gourmet shops. Bloomingdale's sells Magic Mommy bread in all five of its branch stores.

Specialty items from Magic Mommy include animal sculptures, a bread basket filled with little mushrooms, and a twenty-pound mushroom bread that can be used for a party.

Magic Mommy will soon be conducting tours of her kitchens for people interested in baking bread. Baking classes for children will also be held on the premises in the future.

Top: Dough being kneaded.
Finished bread is weighed.
Bread is removed from mold.
Bottom: Glazing mushroom bread with butter.
Bread cooling.
Glazing loaves.

Olsen's is known for
Swedish limpa,
mellen bread, and
kneip bread

Olsen's Bakery, in Brooklyn, makes all its special Scandinavian breads with natural ingredients. Norwegian food stores and some delicatessens, as well as Olsen's itself, sell Scandinavian kneip bread (light pumpernickel) and verter, hvete and milke kakes (special sweet breads).

This Scandinavian bakery has existed for some time, but Thoralf Olsen and his family have only run it for six years.

Roy Olsen, Thoralf's son, helps his father in the store each night. The bakery employs eight bakers and six other people to work inside the shop.

Although the baker's products are mostly Scandinavian, Thoralf Olsen himself came to the United States from Norway. He bakes Swedish Limpa (long loaf) and a special light rye bread, in addition to the Scandinavian products for which his bakery is famous.

Olsen's Bakery
5722 8th Avenue
Brooklyn, N.Y.
212/GE 9-6673

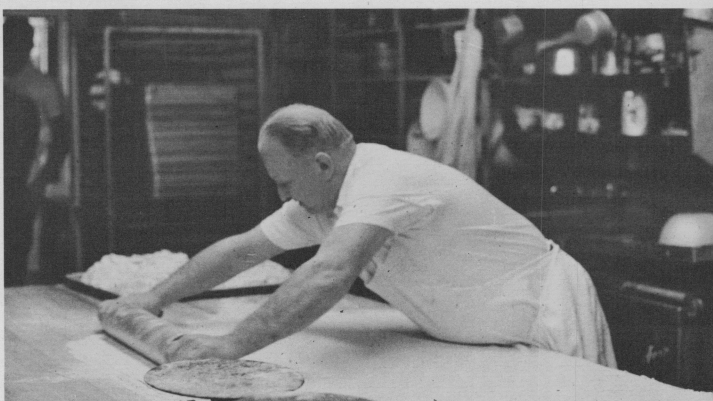

To make his Scandinavian specialties, Olsen's bakers first weigh the dough. Next it is kneaded, then rolled out, and placed in baking pans. The top of each loaf is scored and coated. Finally, the bread goes into the oven.

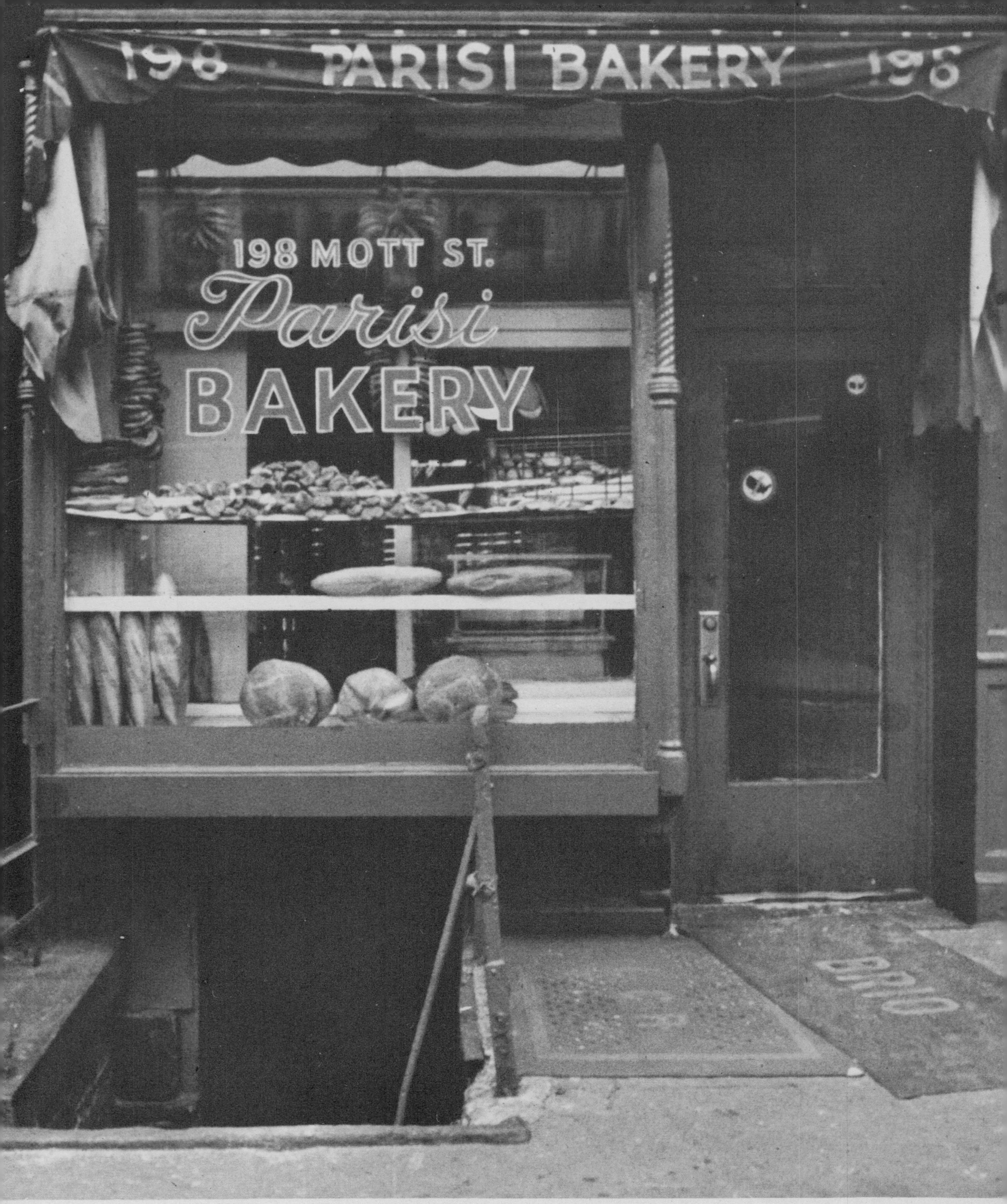
198 PARISI BAKERY 198
198 MOTT ST.
Parisi
BAKERY

baking means life to the Parisi family

Parisi Bakery
198 Mott Street
New York, New York
212/CA 6-6378

Sixty-one years ago, Vincent Parisi opened a bakery which has belonged to his family ever since. His son Joseph, and Joseph's son Robert (the current owner), have kept the special original flavor of Parisi's bread alive for more than half a century. And when Robert's two sons, Frank and George, are old enough, the Parisi bakery will belong to them.

This old-style family bakery produces about 5000 loaves of bread each day. It is open 24 hours a day, and work is done in two shifts; from 9 AM to 3 PM and from 3 PM to 6 AM.

Seven different types of bread are baked at Parisi's: butter bread, sweet bread, regular french bread, long french bread, apolidian round bread, seeded french bread and whole wheat bread.

Two of Parisi's most famous recipes are for seeded french bread and whole wheat bread.

Seeded French Bread
1/2–1 cup of water
3 oz. salt
1/4 lb. yeast
Hecker's white flour
Knead bread, then let rise for one hour. Shape into long hot-dogs. Let rise again, add sesame seeds to top half, creating center line. Bake in oven at 350° for 25–30 minutes.

Whole Wheat Bread
1/2–1 cup water
3 oz. salt
1/4 lb. yeast
whole wheat flour
Knead bread at room temperature for 1/2 hour. Then shape bread in greased pan and let rise for 25 minutes. Then bake in 350° oven for 25-30 minutes.

Peggy Lehrecke
Whole Grain Bread

Our family has always considered baking bread one of the basic human activities. My most vivid memory of Grandma Bosworth's farm kitchen is the huge, black woodburning stove which never went cold. During the day the warming oven provided the best possible rising conditions for sweet-smelling loaves and cinnamon buns; during the night the enormous earthenware pitchers with yeast batter for the breakfast hot cakes sat quietly on the back of the warm stove, miraculously fermenting while the family slept. My other grandmother was raised on a farm close to the Gettysburg battlefield, where the rich soil produced both hard and soft wheat of high quality. The very best spring grains were saved for the Communion bread, baked weekly in the outdoor brick oven. According to a very "high" liturgical tradition among those Scotch Calvinist farmers, a ritual developed around the baking on Saturday, the Communion on Sunday, and the distribution of the remaining bread among the congregation after the service.

All of this was believed to sanctify the common life and labor and to relate the gifts of the earth to the gifts of faith.

I began baking immediately after returning to the States from several years in Europe. My continental husband could scarcely be expected to tolerate the "non-food" masquerading under the name of bread in this land of plenty, and my own background clearly left no question as to how the need should be met. I started with crusty French or Italian loaves from unbleached flour with wheat germ added. Then gradually I turned increasingly to whole grains as I became more aware of the central position bread was assuming in the diet of my growing family. In order to enjoy the freshest, most nutritious flour, I decided to invest in an electrically-powered stone mill, which was soon paid for by selling bread to neighbors. That was almost fifteen years ago, and the whole-grain habit has persisted. The product is never quite the same twice, since we like to try different combinations of grains. If the procedure looks

frightfully long, do not lose heart. Most of the work-hours are put in by yeast and oven. Your own involvement is limited and flexible. The heavenly smell from the kitchen, the exciting feeling of yeast dough coming to life in your hands, the nose-tingling fascination of experimenting with a sourdough pot, and above all the pleasure of the fresh loaf ---- these will provide more than enough rewards for the time spent.

Equipment: if you are serious about your bread, you will probably find it worth your while to bake in serious quantities. Even if you do not have a large family, the list of friends hoping and hinting for loaves will grow weekly. I bake three loaves at a time, each weighing about three pounds. This assumes the following equipment:
1. 3 long loaf pans, sometimes sold as angel cake pans; mine measure 4-1/2" x 4-1/2" x 16".
2. A large mixing bowl; earthenware offers the most even warmth, but the larger sizes of Japanese enamelware do very well.
3. A large paddle-shaped wooden mixing spoon.

4. An earthenware crock (or bean pot) for nursing along and storing your sourdough culture, large enough for 3 quarts.
5. Rubber scrapers for keeping the inside of your sourdough pot tidy.

Preparation: for your sourdough starter, you can either beg a half a cup from a friend or start from scratch. *The Joy of Cooking* has a good starter recipe, as do many other standard cookbooks. If this is your first experience with sourdough, remember some of the time-honored rules:
1. Keep your crock clean; wash it thoroughly with boiling water once a week.
2. Never increase your quantity more than double. Assume that your friend has given you 1 cup of starter: add 1 cup lukewarm water, stir well, then stir in enough whole grain flour to give your dough the consistency of oatmeal. Be sure that your jar has space for the starter to rise while it ferments. Cover loosely and set in a warm, protected place for 12-24 hours. You may then double the quantity again

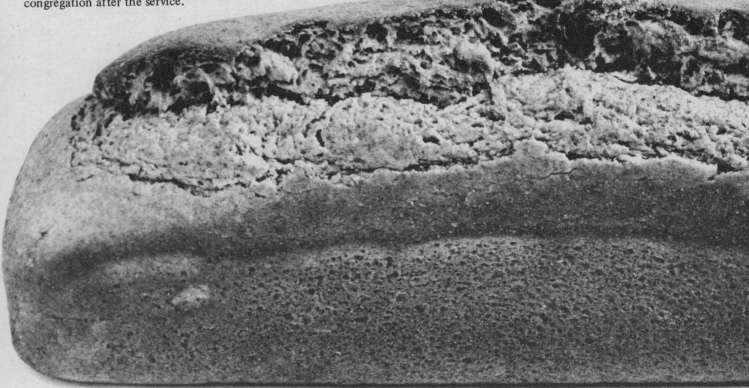

in the same manner, shifting as necessary to larger crocks, until you have about 2-3 quarts of starter. You will have noticed by now that you need several days to prepare your culture before the actual baking begins.

3. After your starter has ripened to the desired degree of sharpness, store in refrigerator until you are ready to bake. This may be from one to three days after your last doubling. The point at which the starter develops a "hooch", that heady green liquid on the surface, depends on temperature, humidity, and other factors. If you like a really sour bread, simply stir in the hooch and proceed with your recipe. On the other hand, if you find that your starter has gone too far, or if you desire a milder flavor, pour out all but one or two cups of the dough and begin the increasing process again. Remember that at any point in the doubling procedure you can halt the process by returning your crock to the refrigerator.

4. Always take out a cup of starter before you begin to prepare each baking. The new starter should not be mixed with milk,

yeast or shortening, but increased as before with flour and water. You will soon find the combination of factors (temperature, ripening time, etc.) which produces your favorite culture. My own starter, reputed to have come from a 75-year-old strain, has been living with us continually now for about seven years, and grows sweeter with age. And now for the baking:

1. Scald one quart of milk. Remove from heat and add 4 tablespoons of butter and 4 tablespoons of honey. When cooled to the proper temperature for yeast, add this too. I prefer "real" chunks of fresh yeast from my local baker. I use about a 1/2" slice from a one pound bar at each baking. If you use dry yeast, 2 or 3 packages should be about right. Mix yeast into milk and put aside in a warm place until mixture is bubbly, about five minutes.

2. While the yeast is dissolving, measure out 6-8 cups of starter into your large mixing bowl. (Be sure that you have saved a cup for the crock to keep your culture going!) Add the bubbly yeast-milk mixture to the bowl, mix well.

3. Add about 7 cups of whole wheat flour to the mixing bowl. (Optional: 1 cup of wheat germ in addition.) With large wooden

paddle, mix together and beat well for about 5 minutes, pulling the dough across the whole bowl with each stroke and turning the bowl as you work. The dough should become smooth, rubbery, and springy to the touch.

4. In a small dish, mix 2 teaspoons of baking powder, 2 tablespoons sugar, and 2 teaspoons salt. Sprinkle on the surface of the batter and mix in lightly. Cover bowl with damp towel and set in a warm, draft-free place, such as an (unheated!) oven or a high closet shelf. After 30-45 minutes the sponge should have risen slightly and developed a foamy look.

5. For the next rising, you may add either whole grain flours (which produces a firm loaf), or unbleached white flour (which produces a lighter-textured loaf), or any combination of flours. Add gradually about 6 cups of flour to the mixing bowl, stirring flour in at first with the paddle, then kneading it in with your right hand while your (clean!) left manages the cup with fresh flour, manipulates water faucets, answers the phone, etc. When the dough breaks away from the sides and is stiff enough for kneading, roll out of mixing bowl onto floured counter. Put your mixing bowl into the sink and fill with cold water; it will soak clean while you proceed with the serious business of kneading.

6. Keeping your supply of flour handy, begin to knead with both hands, adding flour as necessary to keep the dough from sticking to the counter. You will be giving the dough a quarter-turn with each rolling push, folding in and pressing with the "heel" of your hands. With white whole-grain mixtures this may take 10–15 minutes before the dough begins to hold to a ball-like shape and spring back when pressed with a finger. A completely whole-grain dough may take more kneading before reaching that point of elasticity. Stay with it – if your yeast is fresh and your sourdough healthy, you can't miss.

7. When your dough is bouncy and fine-textured, cut it into three pieces of equal size. Put them to rest for 20 minutes on the floured board, separated,

lightly dusted with flour, and covered with a damp towel. Meanwhile:

a. Clean out that mixing bowl now, so it's out of your way.

b. Oil each of the bread pans with a puddle of oil about the size of a silver dollar. Spread the oil over the pans and place convenient to your counter.

8. Pre-heat oven to 400 degrees. Take each of the three dough pieces, knead gently for a few minutes, roll out to correct the length for pan, press into greased pan, and lightly oil surface. Place the three pans in a warm, draft-free corner, covered with the damp towel. In 3/4 to 1-1/2 hours, depending on humidity and temperature, the dough should be almost doubled in bulk. You should remember to make a mental note of the starting bulk. If the dough rises too much, it will collapse during the baking. You should try to pop the pans into the oven just before they have reached the doubled point.

9. Your almost-doubled loaves are now in the middle of the 400-degree oven. You have cleaned off your counter with the help of a pancake turner before the scraps of dough dried.

Your work is done. You pour yourself a glass of wine, put up your feet and bask in the most euphoric aroma this side of heaven. After 15-20 minutes the crust will be slightly browned. Turn the heat down to 350 degrees and bake for another 45–65 minutes. Here you use your own judgment. The loaf must break free from the sides of the pan; it should sound hollow when thumped with a finger. A smaller loaf (4″ high) will be baked through sooner than a higher loaf (6″), a loaf with some white flour sooner than one from whole grain flour. One sure test of doneness is to cut open a loaf; if it is still too moist in the center, return the cut halves to the pan, and all the pans to the oven, for more baking.

10. When you are willing to commit yourself to the (hopefully) finished loaves, take them out of the oven, remove them immediately from the pans, and coat the exposed surfaces with butter. What you don't devour immediately with fresh sweet butter can be stored, frozen, or given away to eager friends.

Edgar Levy
French Bread

My recipe for 4 loaves of
French bread is to combine
about 2 pounds of unbleached
flour, 2 cups of water, 2
tablespoons of salt, and 2
tablespoons of sugar. Add to
this mix one cup of warmish
water in which 2 packages or
cakes of yeast and 1 tablespoon of sugar have been
dissolved. Knead this mixture
well, set it to rise, knock it
down after a few hours,
knead it again—lightly this
time. Let it rest for fifteen
minutes, shape it into loaves,
put them on a greased baking
sheet sprinkled with corn meal,
let them rise for an hour. Bake
them in a good hot oven on
the floor of which a large pan
of water has been placed. Take
them out when they are done,
perhaps in thirty-five minutes,
and let them cool on a rack.

All this is simplicity itself. If
you insist on more specific
instructions look in a cook
book—any cook book.

What strikes me about much
of the home bread making that
goes on now is a self-conscious-
ness that tries to endow the
operation with the qualities of
creative imagination. Forget it.
There are pleasant satisfactions
to be gotten from making one's
own bread but the main one
should be eating it. The precious
mystique would disappear if
that were the defining aspect
of the entire process.

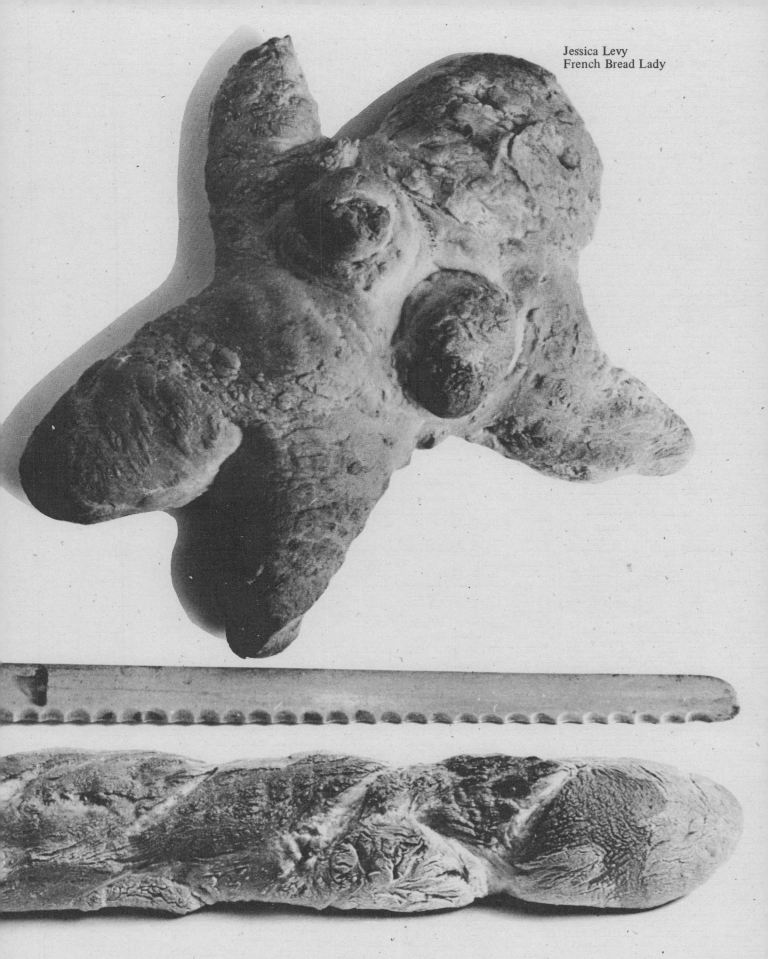

Dorothy Maas
Party Bread

No, said the Little Red Hen. I planted the seed. I tended the grain. I ground the flour. I baked the bread. And now I will eat it myself. And she did.

In so doing, she missed some of the best fringe benefits of bread-making - - the awe and acclaim of one's friends and relatives over the results of what is really a rather minor effort.

A basic requirement for making bread is that you're going to be at home, or near home, for whatever time it takes the bread to get itself ready for the oven. Some breads require more rising time than others, but none should be hurried. This recipe takes at least five hours, and you should allow six, maybe even more if you are making bread for the first time. You'll spend most of the time waiting for the bread to rise, so you can plan other chores. You will need to have in the house the following ingredients and equipment: a three-to-five-pound bag of unbleached white flour, an envelope of dry yeast (or a yeast cake), lard or vegetable shortening, sugar, salt and milk; a large crockery or glass mixing bowl (no plastic bowls, please), one small mixing bowl, a one-quart saucepan, a measuring cup, a wooden mixing spoon, a flour sifter, some waxed paper, several clean dishtowels, two 5"-by-10"loaf pans, or three smaller pans, and a clean, fairly large surface for kneading. You will also require a warm, draft-free place (75 to 85 degrees) in which the bread can rise. I usually place two tea-towel-draped chairs near a warm but not hot radiator. Begin by assembling all your utensils, and greasing the pans well with vegetable shortening or vegetable oil (not olive oil). Then put the following ingredients into the large mixing bowl:
1 tablespoon butter
1 tablespoon lard or shortening
2 tablespoons sugar
2 teaspoons salt
Then put one cup of milk into the saucepan and heat over a medium flame until the surface of the milk begins to steam and move slightly. Add one cup of hot water to the hot milk and pour the milk and water over the ingredients in the mixing bowl. Stir and let cool.
While the milk mixture is cooling, sift, then measure six and one-half cups of the unbleached white flour, using two large sheets of waxed paper for this rather messy operation. After the flour is measured, heat the small mixing bowl with hot water, dry, and pour one-fourth cup of lukewarm water into it and add the envelope of yeast. After the yeast has softened slightly, stir and let stand until the yeast and water mixture becomes thick and bubbly.
When the mixture in the large bowl has cooled to body temperature (try a drop on your wrist), add the yeast mixture,

then (slowly) mix in three
s of flour. Beat the batter for
inute and then add and stir
he remaining flour. You will
e a thick, rather sticky dough.
n this out onto a floured
ace, gather it into a ball, and
er it lightly with a towel
le you wash and butter light-
he large mixing bowl. You
uld also butter your hands.
w you are ready to knead the
d. You do this by pressing
the mass of dough away
n yourself with the heels of
r hands, then folding it to-
d you. Repeat the process
ushing and folding, turning
dough as you work, until it
nooth and elastic — for about
minutes. Add flour to the
ading surface if the bread
s.
r the bread is thoroughly

kneaded, place it in the large
bowl, turning it as you do so in
order to spread a film of butter
over the top. Cover the bowl
with a towel and put the bread
to rise in the warm, draft-free
spot you have prepared. When
the bread has doubled in bulk
(in about an hour), punch it
down with your fist, turn it
over, re-cover, and let it rise for
about an hour and a half, or until it has doubled again.

After it has risen the second
time, the bread is ready for the
pans. Turn it out of the bowl,
let it rest for a few minutes,
then cut it into halves or thirds
and place these in the loaf pans,
tucking the ends to make a
smooth top.

Let it rise once more, uncovered
this time so a crust will form,

until it doubles. While it is rising,
remove one shelf from your oven
and place the remaining shelf in
the lower third (but not in the
lowest slot) of the oven. On the
bottom of the oven, set a large
shallow pan of boiling water.
Then light the oven and heat to
450 degrees.

Bake the bread at 450 for ten
minutes, then reduce the heat
to 350 and bake for about
thirty minutes longer, or until
the bread shrinks from the sides
of the pans and sounds hollow
when tapped. During the baking
process, replenish the boiling
water if necessary. The steam
helps to produce a thick,
crisp crust.

When the bread is baked, remove
the loaves from the pans immediately and set them on a table on

the unused oven shelf (or a cake
rack) to cool. You are not sup-
posed to cut them while they
are warm, but how can you re-
sist?

The bread in the photograph
was made by doubling this recipe and baking it in a huge old
commercial cake pan. It makes
a fine centerpiece for a buffet
table. It may be possible for
you to find similar pans in res-
taurant supply houses (mine
came from an antique store),
but I suggest practicing with
smaller pans before trying one
big one. After the second rising,
you can also make bread sculptures with this recipe. A third
rising is not then necessary, because handling causes the bread
to rise sufficiently.

Amy Norman
Challah

I started baking bread when I lived in New Mexico and have since collected recipes during my stays in London and San Francisco.

At Kirkland College I took a student-run class in bread baking. I have baked all sorts of breads ranging from yeasted ones to almost cake-like; banana, date nut loaves to name two. Many of the techniques of bread baking closely mirror the methods I use with clay. I like to do both.

1/3 cup oil
1/3 cup sugar
1 cup hot water
5 cups white flour
1 Tablespoon salt
2 eggs, beaten
1 pkg. dry yeast
poppy seeds

1. Dissolve yeast in warm water (1/4 cup).
2. Add salt, sugar, oil, eggs, water and flour (gradually).
3. Mix, stir, knead until dough is smooth and elastic (knead on a floured board).
4. Cover and set aside in a warm place until the dough doubles in size (about 1 1/2 hours). Punch down.
5. Divide into 2 loaves, braid.
6. Let rise for 1 1/2 hours.
7. Brush with beaten egg yolk and sprinkle with poppy seeds.
8. Bake at 350 degrees for 45 minutes in greased pan.

Francesca Burgess
Five Grain Brown Bread

Bread baking is an art I learned from necessity in the days when we lived for awhile far from grocery stores. My first few tries were not successful as bread; but after many false starts I finally managed to bake a loaf that was hearty but not too heavy, that could be sliced thin without falling apart and that tasted equally good with cheese or marmalade or just plain sweet butter. We like it best toasted lightly. Makes three loaves.

In a large warmed mixing bowl put the following:
½ cup malt extract*
2 tablespoons honey
1 tablespoon salt
2 tablespoons shortening
Pour over 2 cups boiling water and stir until dissolved. Add:
1 cup scalded milk, mix well and then 1-1/2 cups of Dr. Jackson's Meal,** and 1 cup of uncooked oatmeal. Cover with a clean cloth and let rest until warm. Prepare 1 1/2 packages of dry yeast in 1/2 cup warm water mixed with a little honey. When the hot cereal mixture has cooled down to comfortably warm, stir in the dissolved yeast. Beat in 3 cups of white (Hecker's) flour, cover with cloth and let rest again for about 20 minutes.

Beat up the dough and add 2 cups of whole wheat flour. Again cover and let rest 20 minutes or half an hour, in medium temperature away from drafts.

Work in 2 more cups of whole wheat flour, using hands and kneading on pastry board or marble slab. Halfway through the kneading, roll the dough into a ball, cover with towel and let it rest awhile. During this time wash out the mixing bowl, rinse in hot water and butter it well. Continue kneading the dough adding the final bit of flour slowly, until the dough is elastic and no longer sticks to your hands. Shape it into a smooth ball. Roll it around in the buttered warm bowl and set it seam side down to rise. Cover with a piece of plastic wrap and a towel. Let it rise in a moderate temperature, out of drafts, until double, about 1 1/2 – 2 hours. Then punch it down with your fist, form into a neat ball, turn it over so that the seam side is down and cover again to rise a second time. Grease three bread pans. After the second rising, divide the dough into 3 parts, form into long rolls to fit the pans, again having all seams underneath, cover and let rise until double. By this time you're probably in a hurry to get the whole process finished, but be very careful not to let the loaves rise too fast or too high or there will be great holes inside, and if the bread rises in too hot a place there will be a hard, thick crust on the bottom. If you decide to set it on top of the oven while it is heating, be sure to set it on cake racks, and cover with the plastic wrap and towel.
Bake 45 minutes in a 375-degree oven. When the bread is done it will sound hollow when tapped on the bottom, and will easily come out of the pan.
For a soft crust, butter tops of loaves as they come from the oven, then set loaves on their sides to cool on racks.

---

*Pabst Blue Ribbon Malt Extract is sold in health food stores. You may have to look around for it— ask them to order it. It's really intended for making home-brew. It comes in 3-pound cans. Measure it at room temperature. It is extremely thick and sticky and is hard to measure in a cup. I use an old silver serving spoon which is plunged into the malt and then pulled out, and twirled around until the malt is one lump on the spoon. This should be about the right amount. You may want to measure this quantity the first time. There is really no substitute for this malt—it is the secret ingredient.

**Dr. Jackson's Meal is in most health food stores.

Magda Surmach
Ukrainian Easter Paska

The Ukrainian paska is the traditional bread at Easter breakfast for millions of Ukrainians
who still celebrate Easter in a
tradition that is at least one
thousand years old.

1 tsp. sugar
1/2 cup lukewarm water
1 pkg. granular yeast
1 1/2 cups scalded milk, lukewarm
2 1/2 cups sifted flour
4 eggs, beaten
1/3 cup sugar
1/3 cup melted butter
2 tsp. salt
5 cups sifted flour

Dissolve 1 tsp. sugar in lukewarm water and sprinkle yeast
over it. Let stand in warm place
for 10 minutes. Combine the
softened yeast with the lukewarm milk and 2 1/2 cups flour.
Beat well until smooth. Cover
and let batter rise in warm place
until light and bubbly. Add the
beaten eggs, sugar, melted butter,
salt; mix thoroughly. Stir in 5
cups of flour. Knead until the
dough no longer sticks to hands
and is smooth and satiny—15
to 20 minutes. Replace in bowl,
cover and let rise in warm place
until double in bulk. Punch
down and let rise again.
Divide dough into 2 parts re-
serving small portion for the
decorations. Pans should be
round and pretty tall. Oven-
proof small pots or empty coffee
cans will do nicely. Grease pans
and sprinkle with flour on the
inside. Dough should not take
up more than 1/3 of the pan.
Allow to rise to double bulk
and then decorate.
To decorate: roll out unused
portion of dough into as many
"long rolls" as you think you
will need for the type of decor-
ation you wish to make. For the
traditional cross on the Ukrainian Easter Babka you will, of
course, need two long pieces per
paska. To make the cross more
decorative you can split the ends
and curl them under as seen in
the illustration.
Place paskas into 400-degree
oven and bake for 10 minutes.
Reduce heat to 350 degrees and
continue baking for 35 - 40 minutes. If the tops brown too
quickly, cover loosely with al-
uminum foil. During the last
five minutes of baking, brush
paskas with beaten egg diluted
with milk or water.

52

alyn Kaufman
other's Bread

r me the whiff of bread fresh
om the oven carries with it
o vivid mental pictures: a tree-
ed small-town street in Mich-
an, fragrant with the smell of
ead wafting across the lawn to
eet me as I came home from
hool; and, once in the back
or, the sight of plump, golden
aves and a swirl of pungent
nnamon buns cooling on the
g kitchen table, spotlighted by
e afternoon sun. Delicious
ages and delicious bread.

why did it take me so long to
ke bread myself? I honestly
n't know, but on a Thanksgiv-
g visit to my parents two years
o I sat my 86-year-old mother
wn in a kitchen chair next to
e table (same kitchen, same
ble) and under her direction I
embled all the ingredients,
d mixed and kneaded bread
ugh for the first time in my
e. To my amazement, the
ugh rose beautifully in little
re than an hour. My mother
owed me how to punch down
dough, and shape the loaves
the second rise, also without
itch. I put them in her 50-year
bread tins, which she never
shes, just wipes clean. And the
ad was great — just like

mother used to make it. I was
hooked. From then on I bake
bread not regularly but often.
Once I got interested, I started
reading bread recipes and study-
ing cookbooks and finding out
more about bread baking. Gradually I began to experiment with
the family loaf which calls for
all-white flour. When I tried sub-
stituting half whole-wheat flour,
the first loaf was too solid, and
heavy, but very good neverthe-
less. Then I read somewhere that
when you use whole-wheat flour,
you should add a little more
liquid. When I did that (adding
about 1/4 cup of water to the
amount in the original recipe)
the bread was perfect.
When I am in the bread-baking
mood I resort to the family
recipe, making it either all-white
or half and half, because I am
sure of it, and everyone likes it.
Here are a few things I have
learned that may be worth pass-
ing along:
At first follow a reliable recipe
faithfully. Don't change any-
thing. Experiment later, after
you know how to make that
bread and know what you would
like to change.

Let bread rise in a warm (not hot)
sheltered place. Too much heat
can kill the yeast.

Don't be afraid of the dough. Let
it know who's boss. Over-knead
rather than under-knead.
Keep baking. Bread baking is an
experience too good to miss.

Mother's Bread
This makes two loaves in pans
about 8x4-1/2x2-1/2 inches*
(to make one loaf, cut each ingredient in half).
Ingredients:
3/4 cup warm water
2 envelopes dry yeast **
1 cup scalded milk, allowed to
cool slightly, but still warm
1 heaping tablespoon margarine
3 tablespoons sugar
2 teaspoons salt
1/2 cup warm water
flour: 2 cups sifted white all-
purpose flour; 2 cups unsifted
whole wheat flour; plus about
1 cup more of unsifted white
flour (a variable amount)
Sprinkle the yeast into 1/2 cup
warm (not hot) water in a large
bowl that you can mix the dough
in. Scald the milk and add to it
the margarine. Set aside to cool
slightly or set it briefly into a
pan of cool water; then add the
warm milk mixture to the dissolved yeast. Add the sugar, salt
and remaining 1/2 cup of warm
water. Stir together with a rubber
spatula or spoon. Add the four
cups of white and whole wheat

flour to the liquid mixture a
little at a time, mixing with a
spoon between each addition.
Add enough of the extra cup of
white flour to make the dough a
sticky mass that you can turn out
on a floured board (if too runny
you won't be able to knead it).
Before you start kneading,
grease a large bowl (3 times larger than the dough) with margarine.

To knead: dust your hands lightly
with flour. Push the mass of dough
away from you with heels of your
hands, then pull it back toward
you. When the dough sticks, add
a little more white flour underneath; add very little at a time,
only as needed to keep dough
from sticking. Dust your hands
with flour as they become sticky.
Knead for at least 10 minutes,
then about 5 minutes more.
Kneading improves the texture.
When dough is ready for rising,
it will have a smooth shiny texture, and will no longer stick to
the board as you work it. Place
the neat ball of dough in the
greased bowl and flop it over so
the top will be greased. Cover the
bowl with a clean towel and set
it in a sheltered, warm (not hot)
corner to rise. If it is drafty or
cool in the room, set the bowl in
an unlighted oven with a pan of
warm water underneath. Let it
rise until double in bulk. To test
this: push two fingers lightly into
the top; if indentations stay, the
dough has doubled in bulk. This
should take from 1 to 1 1/2 hours,
depending on the liveliness of
your yeast, and on temperature
conditions.
Form into two balls and let them
rest about 5 minutes. Shape each
into a loaf. Place the seam
underneath in the pan; grease the
tops lightly with margarine.***
Let rise until double in bulk.
These should be covered. Bake for
1 hour in an oven preheated to
375 degrees. When you think the
bread should be done, give it a
little rap on top with your
knuckles and it will sound hollow. It also will slide out of the
pan easily. Let it cool on a rack.

---

*Present-day standard bread pans
are 9¼ x 5½ x 3, too large for
this recipe. There is an oblong
Pyrex dish that is the right size.
**Make sure the yeast is fresh; check
the dates on the envelopes.
***You can slash the bread across
the top with the tip of a very
sharp knife or razor blade.

53

Gayle Clark
Whole Wheat Bread

2 envelopes active dry yeast
3 1/4 cup warm water
1/2 cup sugar
1 1/4 tablespoons salt
3 1/2 cup whole wheat flour
3 1/2 cup unbleached flour

1. Dissolve yeast in 1/4 cup warm
water with 1 tablespoon sugar.
2. Place flour, sugar, salt, and water
in large bowl. Add yeast mixture.
Make a soft dough. If too sticky,
add more flour (white). Knead on a
floured board and place in greased
bowl until double in size.
3. Punch down; knead, let rise again
until double in size.
4. Punch down; knead. Place in
bread pans, fill pan 3/4 of the way,
let rise again until dough rises to
top of pan.
5. Bake at 400 degrees
for 30-35 minutes.

Gayle Clark
Challah Recipe

2 envelopes dry active yeast
2/3 cup sugar plus 1/2 teaspoon
7 3/4 cups unbleached flour
2 1/4 cups warm water
1/2 cup oil
2 tablespoons salt
3 eggs

1. Place yeast, a little sugar in 3/4 cup warm water.
2. Place 4 cups flour, 1 1/2 cups warm water, 1/2 cup oil, 2/3 cup sugar, the salt and 2 1/2 eggs, mix well.
3. Add yeast to batter. Gradually add 3 more cups flour. Knead in bowl. Cover and set in warm place until double in size.
4. Punch down, knead and cover until double in size.
5. Punch down, knead, place in bread pans or shape in loaves.
6. Cover, let rise. Brush over tops of breads with the remaining egg and 1/2 teaspoon sugar.
7. Sprinkle with poppy seeds and bake at 310 degrees for 45 minutes.

Cleo Fitch
Egg Bread

2 cups water-ground cornmeal
1 teaspoon salt
3 teaspoons of baking powder
Mix these together and add
3/4 cup of milk
2 eggs, beaten lightly
1/4 cup melted butter
Mix and pour into well-buttered
pie pan and bake in 400-degree
oven for about 25 to 30 minutes.

This is a good mix for muffins or
corn sticks. If iron muffin or corn
stick pans are used, they should
be heated first before putting in
mixture.

Hot breads were an important
part of southern meals, and
usually there were hot biscuits
and a hot corn bread for dinner.

Frieda S. Gates
Extra-Healthy Whole Wheat Bread

2 tablespoons organic yeast
2 cups warm water
(about 110—115 degrees)
1/4 cup blackstrap molasses
Combine molasses and water,
sprinkle in yeast, stir lightly.
Place in warm spot to allow yeast
to grow. Meanwhile:
combine 1 beaten egg and 1/4
cup of safflower oil. Add
1 tablespoon salt
1/2 cup powdered milk
1 1/2 cup whole wheat flour
(stone ground)
1 cup soy flour
1/3 cup wheat germ
2 tablespoons brewer's yeast

When yeast mixture has grown
light and fluffy, add to flour mixture. Stir batter until smooth.

Add 2 1/2 to 3 cups more flour
(use white or whole wheat or a
combination). Blend in a little at
a time to form a smooth soft
dough. Knead briefly till dough
is smooth and elastic.
Remove dough from bowl and
oil bowl. Replace dough and
cover with cloth or foil. Place
bowl in a warm spot (80 to 85 F.)
to rise, 45 to 60 minutes.
Punch down dough. Divide in
half. Shape into 2 loaves. Place
in greased pans. Brush tops with
melted butter or margarine (soy
margarine is best), sprinkle with
sesame seeds. Cover: let rise in
warm spot 50 to 60 minutes.

Preheat oven 350 F. Bake 40 to
45 minutes until loaf sounds
hollow when lightly tapped on
bottom of pan. Remove from
pan immediately. Cool on rack.

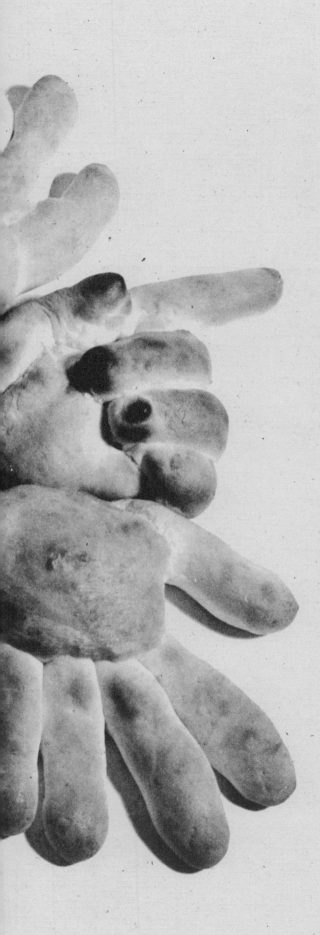

Christine Russo
Fastnacht (Fast Night) Bread

This is the original recipe as it was in my mother's cookbook. It makes 10 dozen.

1 cup unsalted mashed potatoes (about two medium potatoes)
1 quart potato water (the water the potatoes were cooked in)
1 cup lard
2 eggs
2 teaspoons salt
1 cup sugar
1 cake of yeast
4 quarts of flour

There were no other instructions, but after the dough had risen, it was rolled out with enough flour to keep it from sticking to the bread board, about 3/8″ and then cut in oblongs about 2″x4″, and when these strips had raised again they were deep fried, drained on paper and sprinkled with sugar. They are delicious raised doughnuts. My mother, Katerina Hoff, always made these Fastnachts early on the morning of Shrove Tuesday and we took them to her two brothers' families in time for breakfast. She mixed the dough the night before. It was a custom handed down from her parents who came here from Germany.

I like to play around with recipes and have changed it a bit to make the bread hands.

Potato Bread

1 cup mashed potatoes (unsalted)
1 cup margarine or butter
1 1/2 tablespoons salt
1 cake of yeast (or 1 package of dry yeast)
1 quart potato water
2 eggs
1/4 cup sugar
4 quarts flour (16 cups)

Boil two medium-sized potatoes in about a quart of water until they are tender. If you cut them in small pieces they will cook more quickly. Drain the liquid off into a bowl. (I usually measure it as I drain it—saves rehandling the liquid.) If there aren't 4 cups, add enough water to make that much. Take 1/4 cup of this liquid, dissolve the sugar in it and either crumble the 1 cake of yeast in it or if you are using the packaged dry yeast sprinkle it in and stir it a couple of turns (use your finger, saves washing a spoon — I hope you started with clean hands). It's important that the water you dissolve the yeast in is not too hot; that's the reason I stir it with my finger – if the water is just warm to my finger it will be just right for the yeast, but if it's too hot for my finger it's too hot for the yeast—it won't rise.

Set this mixture aside while you mash the potatoes. To the potato water, add the margarine (cut in slices as it will melt more quickly), the salt, and the mashed potatoes.

Set aside to cool a bit. In a big pan (I use an old, large broiler pan) measure the flour and when the potato water mixture is lukewarm to your finger, make a hole in the center of the flour and pour the mixture into the hole, along with the dissolved yeast and the eggs. Stir with one hand, pulling the flour into the middle a little at a time, until it gets thick, then start kneading the rest of the flour into the mixture until you get it all worked in and the dough gets smooth and satiny and is slightly elastic. (If the dough is sticky on your hands, just dip your hands in a bit of flour and rub them together and the dough will rub off in pieces.) Take about 2 tablespoons of margarine or butter and rub around the pan and over the dough, so when it rises it will not get crusty. Cover and let set in a warm place to rise. When it is double in size, it is time to start forming the hands — or loaves if you wish. To get the hands to retain their shape I did not let them rise the second time, but baked them after letting them set only about ten minutes.

But forming them into loaves and letting them double in bulk before baking them improves the texture and flavor. Using a bit of margarine will keep the dough from sticking to your hands. To make a hand, roll each finger a bit longer and a bit thinner than your finger and make the palm a bit smaller and a bit thinner than the palm of your hand. To make a loaf use an amount of dough about half the size of the finished loaf you desire. Bake in a 400-425-degree oven until browned and the dough is loose from the baking pan. If you like a crusty crust, put a pan of water in the bottom of your oven while baking, but if you like a soft crust, brush the baked loaf with margarine or butter as it comes out of the oven. Baking bread is a fun thing--so have fun!

Michael J. Rufino
Easter Bread

2 pkgs. yeast
1 cup sugar
4 tsp. salt
1 quart milk
½ lb. butter
8 large eggs or 12 small ones
5 lbs. flour

In small bowl, mix yeast and 1
tsp. sugar in one-third cup
water. Dissolve. In a large bowl,
mix milk, sugar, salt, eggs
(slightly beaten), butter and
dissolved yeast. Add flour, 2
cups at a time. Knead. Let
stand two hours. Punch down.
Let stand 1 hour; punch down.
Form loaves and let stand
another hour. Bake at 375
degrees until done. Will bake to
a nice color.

Roger Shepherd
Cornell Whole-Wheat Bread

Developed in the 40's by the late Dr. Clive M. McCay of Cornell.
For optimum taste and quality use natural and/or organic products wherever possible.

4 cups lukewarm water
4 packages dry active yeast (4 tablespoons)
1/2 cup dark molasses
1/2 cup brown sugar
2 eggs
9 cups (approx.) whole-wheat flour (organic & stone-ground)
1 cup full-fat soy flour
1 1/2 cups nonfat dry milk
6 tablespoons wheat germ
4 tablespoons brewer's yeast
4 teaspoons salt
melted butter (optional)

1. Place the water, yeast, molasses and sugar in a large bowl and let stand for five minutes.

2. Beat in the eggs and 7 cups of whole-wheat flour. Beat the mixture three minutes with an electric beater or 100 strokes by hand.

3. Mix together the remaining ingredients except for the butter. Work the dry ingredients into the yeast mixture and add enough extra flour to make a dough that can be kneaded.

4. Knead the dough until it is smooth and satiny, about 10 minutes. Place in a clean greased bowl, grease the top of the dough and cover and let rise in a warm place until doubled in bulk, about one hour.

5. Punch down, cover and let rest 10 minutes. Divide in thirds and shape each third into a loaf as follows: Roll out one ball into a rectangle twice as big as an 8 1/2 by 4 1/2 by 2 1/2 inch loaf pan. Fold the long sides into the center. Fold short sides to the center. Pinch to seal layers and fit into a greased loaf pan. Repeat with other two balls.

Cover and let rise until double in bulk, about 30 minutes.

6. Preheat oven to 350 degrees. Bake loaves for 50 minutes to an hour or until they sound hollow when tapped on the bottom. Brush tops with melted butter for a soft crust and cool on a rack. For the bread pictured here, the entire dough (normally yielding 3 loaves) was separated into three 4-foot strands and braided. Then the braid was coiled from the center outward, the loose end being tucked back into the braid. An extra 15 minutes baking time was necessary due to the extra volume of the loaf.

Janet Kusmierski and
Paul Castelano
Los Angeles Unyeasted Bread

4 cups of whole wheat flour
3½ cups of brown rice
1 tbs. salt
3½ cups warm water as needed
to make kneadable

Mix ingredients. Knead 300
times (count them). Cover with
wet towel and let sit 12–24
hours in a warm place. Knead
100 times, put in oiled 13 x 9½
x 2-inch pan. Cut top length-
wise and let set 4 hours in a
warm place or 1½ hours in 100-
to 150-degree oven. Bake at 350
degrees for ½ hour, then turn
oven up to 400 degrees for 45
to 60 minutes. The crust should
be dark brown.
Variations:
1. use 4 cups whole wheat flour,
3 cups unbleached white flour.
2. Use 4 cups whole wheat
flour, 3 cups rye or barley
flour.
3. Use 4 cups whole wheat
flour, 2 cups rye, 1 cup corn
millet.
4. You may also substitute
buckwheat flour 1½ cups. The
rest may be either rye or corn
meal with 4 cups whole wheat.
5. Use 4 cups whole wheat
flour, up to 2 cups corn meal,
millet meal, rolled oats.
6. You can add 2-6 tbs. oil per
loaf as a variation.

Kim Elam
Banana Bread*

1) Blend until creamy:
1/3 cup shortening
2/3 cup sugar
3/4 tsp. lemon rind
2) Beat in: 1 egg
3) Sift before measuring
1 1/3 cups flour
4) Resift with
2 tsp. baking powder
1/4 tsp. baking soda

This recipe is originally
from *The Joy of Cooking*.

5) Mash: 2-4 fully ripened
bananas for 1 cup pulp
6) Add sifted ingredients in 3
parts to sugar mixture, alter-
nating with banana pulp.
7) Beat after each addition
until smooth.
8) Place in greased bread pan,
4 in. x 8 in.
9) Bake in preheated oven at
350 degrees for 1 hour.
10) For variation, add 1 cup
raisins, dried prunes, apricots
or nuts.

Louie Valle
Louie's Garlic Pizza Bread

2 pkg. active dry yeast
3/4 cup warm water
2 2/3 cups warm water
1 tbs. salt
3 tbs. shortening
9 cups unbleached white flour
Garlic — 1/4 cup oil, salt and
pepper.

Dissolve yeast in 3/4 cup warm
water. Stir in 2 2/3 cups water,
the salt, and shortening with 5
cups of the flour. Beat until

smooth. Mix in enough flour
to make dough easy to handle.
Turn dough onto lightly
floured board; knead until elastic. Place in greased bowl. Turn
greased side up. Cover and let
rise 1 hour. Punch down and
divide in half. Smooth out one
half of dough onto greased
pizza tin. Cut up 2 cloves of
garlic and sprinkle on dough.
Add salt and pepper and drizzle
1/4 cup corn oil. Bake in preheated oven at 400 degrees for
25 minutes until golden brown.
Add sliced mushrooms for a
variation.

Carlos Darquea and
Amy Braydon
Sweet and Sour Bread

¼ oz. yeast
6 cups unbleached flour
3 tbs. sugar
1½ tsp. salt
3 tbs. butter
3 eggs
1 cup boiling water
1 cup milk
½ cup raisins

Mix package of yeast with ½ cup of warm water, then let it set in separate bowl. In mixing bowl, mix 1 cup of water with 3 tbs. of butter. Let melt. Add 1 cup of warm milk. Add the sugar and salt, add lightly beaten eggs and yeast mixture. Start mixing the flour gradually, stirring constantly. Collect the dough and place in shallow pan. cover. Set for 30 minutes, or until it rises. Knead the dough to any shape desired. Cover and let sit for 30 minutes or more. Preheat oven at 375 degrees. When ready place dough in greased pan and let bake for 40 minutes.

Bill Barrett
Wheat Germ Bread

2 cups milk
2 tsp. butter
2 tsp. salt
¼ cup molasses
¼ cup honey
2 pkgs. yeast
1 cup wheat germ
2¾ cup graham flour
2¾ cup white flour

Scald 2 cups milk. Place in bowl to cool. Add 2 tsp. butter, 2 tsp. salt, ¼ cup molasses, and ¼ cup honey. Dissolve yeast in ½ cup water. Add wheat germ to milk mixture. When cool, add yeast, then flour. Knead for 10 minutes until springy (more flour may be needed). Let rise until almost double in bulk. Knead again and put in loaf pans. Let rise again until almost double. Bake about 35 minutes, 375 degrees. Remove from pans and brush with butter. Return to oven for 10 minutes. Remove. Cool on racks.

Judith Gilmartin
Passion Fruit Cornbread

1½ cups milk
1 cup corn meal
1½ tbs. shortening
2 eggs
1½ tsp. baking powder
½ tsp. salt
2 tsp. sugar
1 tbs. olive juice
10 olives chopped and added to batter

Scald milk, pour over corn meal and shortening. Cool. Add beaten eggs, baking powder, salt, sugar, and olives with juice. Mix well. Pour into cake ring. Make sure pan is well greased. Bake in preheated oven, 400 degrees, for 25 to 30 minutes.

Bonnie Weber
Cinnamon Bread

2 pkgs. active dry yeast or 2 cakes compressed yeast
¼ cup water
1 cup milk scalded
½ cup sugar
1 tbs. salt
¼ cup shortening
5½ to 6 cups sifted enriched flour
2 eggs
2 tbs. melted butter
1 tbs. cinnamon
1/3 cup sugar

Soften active dry yeast in warm water (110 degrees), compressed yeast in lukewarm water 85 degrees. Scald milk. Add ½ cup sugar, salt and shortening. Cool to lukewarm. Add 2 cups flour and mix well. Add softened yeast and eggs; beat well. Add enough flour to make a soft dough. Turn out on lightly floured surface and knead until smooth and elastic (10 minutes). Place in lightly greased bowl, turning once to grease surface. Cover; let rise in a warm place until doubled, about 2 hours. When light, punch down. Divide into two equal portions into a smooth ball. Cover and let rest 10 minutes. Roll each portion into a long, narrow rectangle about ¼ in. thick, 6 by 20 inches. Brush with 2 tbs. melted butter. Sprinkle with mixture of 1 tbs. cinnamon and 1/3 cup sugar. Roll like jelly roll. Seal ends.

Place in two greased bread pans 8½x4½x2½ inches. Brush tops of loaves with melted butter.

Let rise until almost tripled. Place in warm place 1 hr. and 15 minutes. Sprinkle 1 tbs. sugar-cinnamon mixture over top of each loaf. Bake in moderate oven for 45 to 50 minutes.

Clara Parra
Pan de Manteca—Cuban Bread

1 oz. yeast
1 qt. water
3½ lbs. (14 cups) unbleached flour.
1 tbs. salt
6 oz. melted lard
2 tbs. sugar
1 egg yolk

Mix yeast, water (spring water if possible) and 8 cups flour. Cover. Let stand for 3 hours. Yeast mixture will double. Add 1½ lbs. (6 cups) flour and salt, melted lard, sugar. Mix well. Knead thoroughly for 10 minutes. Form 5 loaves approximately 16 inches x 1 inch high x 2 inches wide. Let stand 15 minutes. Brush with egg yolk. Bake at 500 degrees for 1¼ hour or until golden. Yields 5 loaves.

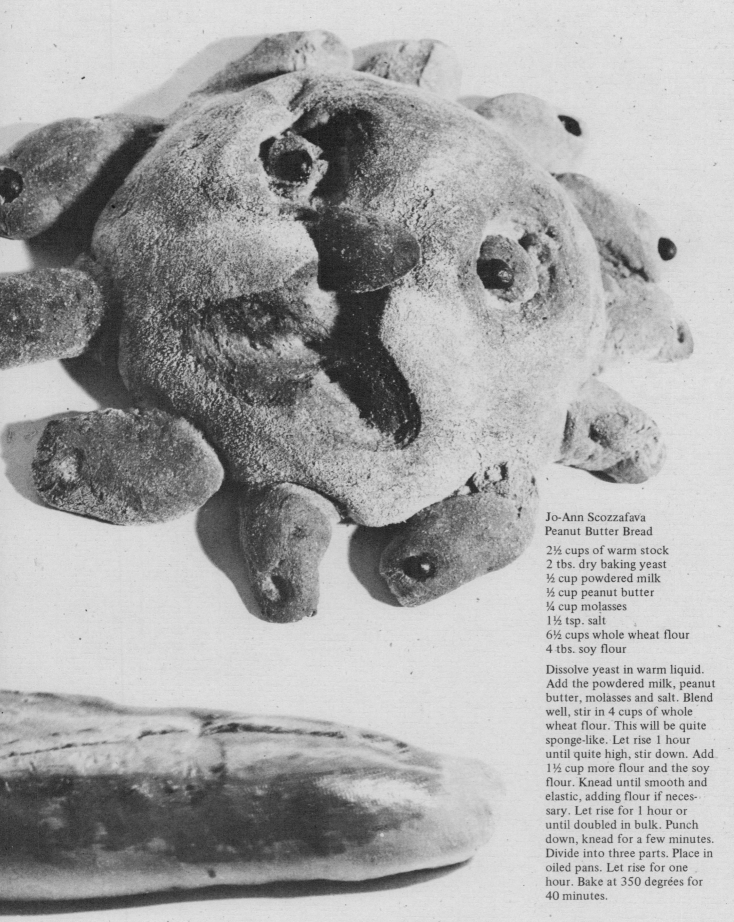

Jo-Ann Scozzafava
Peanut Butter Bread

2½ cups of warm stock
2 tbs. dry baking yeast
½ cup powdered milk
½ cup peanut butter
¼ cup molasses
1½ tsp. salt
6½ cups whole wheat flour
4 tbs. soy flour

Dissolve yeast in warm liquid. Add the powdered milk, peanut butter, molasses and salt. Blend well, stir in 4 cups of whole wheat flour. This will be quite sponge-like. Let rise 1 hour until quite high, stir down. Add 1½ cup more flour and the soy flour. Knead until smooth and elastic, adding flour if necessary. Let rise for 1 hour or until doubled in bulk. Punch down, knead for a few minutes. Divide into three parts. Place in oiled pans. Let rise for one hour. Bake at 350 degrées for 40 minutes.

Jo-Ann Scozzafava
Mixing Bowl Bread

1 pkg. yeast
½ cup warm water
1/8 tsp. ground ginger
3 tbs. sugar
1 can evaporated milk
1 tsp. salt
2 tbs. salad oil
4-4½ cups unsifted flour

Dissolve yeast in water with
ginger and 1 tbs. sugar. Let
stand for fifteen minutes or
until bubbly. Stir in remaining
sugar, milk, salt, oil. Beat flour
in; stir in last cup with
spoon. Flour should be stiff
and heavy, too sticky to knead.
Put in greased bowl, let stand
for 1 hour. Punch down and
knead. Shape on cookie sheet and
let rise about 45 minutes. Bake at
350 degrees for 35 to 45 minutes.
Brush the top with butter and
let cool for ten minutes.

James Cook
Mrs. Kane's Irish Soda Bread

cups sifted flour
tbs. baking powder
tsp. baking soda
tsp. salt
to 3 tbs. sugar (optional)
tbs. wheat germ (optional)
tbs. caraway seeds
to 1 cup raisins
1/3 cup buttermilk

Combine first seven ingredients.
Add raisins. Pour milk into
flour, stir into a ball with a rubber spatula. Spill on to a
floured surface. With floured
hands, flatten dough with your
palms (add flour if dough is
sticky). Continue to knead
dough, folding a quarter edge
of the dough onto the top and
kneading with the palm of your
hand, continue this way, making quarter turns for about 10
minutes. Place on ungreased
cookie sheet or cake pan. Cut a
large cross on bread with a
sharp knife. Bake at 375 degrees for about 35 to 40 minutes. Test by tapping bread. If
it sounds hollow, it's done.

Pete Mattes
Cheese Casserole Bread

4¾ to 5½ cups unsifted flour
3 tbs. sugar
1 tbs. salt
2 pkgs. active dry yeast
1 cup milk
1 cup water
2 tbs margarine
1½ cups grated sharp Cheddar
cheese
1 egg at room temperature

In a large bowl thoroughly mix
1¾ cups flour, sugar, salt and
undissolved yeast. Combine
milk, water and margarine in a
saucepan. Heat over low heat
until liquids are warm (margarine does not need to melt).
Gradually add to dry ingredients and beat two minutes at
medium speed with electric
mixer, scraping bowl occasionally. Add cheese, egg and ½ cup
flour, or enough flour to make
a thick batter. Beat at high
speed two minutes, scraping
bowl occasionally. Stir in
enough additional flour to
make a stiff batter. Beat until
well blended. Cover; let rise in
a warm place, free from draft,
until double in bulk, about 40
minutes. Stir batter down.
Beat vigorously, about ½ min-
ute. Turn into a greased 1-
quart casserole. Bake in moderate oven (375 degrees) about
40 to 50 minutes or until done.
Remove from casserole and
cool on wire racks.

Nancy Kaplow
Adobe Bread

¼ cup warm water
1 package active dry yeast
2 tbs. soft butter
1 tsp. salt
4 cups water
4 cups flour

Combine water, yeast, butter, and salt in a large bowl. Add 4 cups water and 4 cups wheat flour. You will probably have to knead in the last cup of flour. You can substitute ¾ cup of honey for 1 cup water. Cover with dry cloth and let sit for one hour. Split into two loaves. Put dough into greased pans, 4½ x 8½ x 2¾ inches and let rise 15 more minutes. Bake at 400 degrees for 50 minutes.

Katharine Chafee
Date-Nut Bread

1 cup very hot water
1 pkg. (8 oz.) dates
½ cup finely chopped nuts
¼ cup shortening
¾ cup brown sugar
1 egg
1 tsp. baking soda
2 cups all-purpose flour
½ tsp. salt

Chop dates into small pieces and combine with nuts. Pour the hot water over and let stand while preparing. Cream shortening and sugar together and add egg. Beat well. Add soda to the water and add that to the shortening mixture. Sift in flour and salt, stirring until well mixed. Grease pan and line with waxed paper. Grease waxed paper lightly so it doesn't stick. Bake at 325 degrees for 1 hour and 20 minutes. Test with cake tester and remove when it comes out clea

Carolyn Sievers
Homemade White Bread

1 cup scalded milk
3 tbs. sugar
1 tbs. salt
2 pkgs. dry yeast
1¼ cups warm water (110°-115°)
2 tbs. soft shortening
6¾ to 7¼ cup sifted all-purpose flour

Scald milk. Pour into a large bowl with the sugar and salt. Cool to lukewarm. Add yeast to warm water. Let stand 3 to 5 min. Stir; add to the milk mixture. Blend in about ½ the flour with the soft shortening. Beat until smooth with mixer or spoon. Stop mixer. Add more flour a little at a time, first with spoon, then with hand until the dough cleans the bowl. Turn onto lightly floured cloth-covered board. Knead until dough becomes smooth and little bubbles can be seen beneath the surface. Place in greased bowl, turning once. Cover and let rise in warm place until doubled—45 to 60 minutes. To check, dent remains when finger is pressed deep into side of dough.

Punch down dough. Turn over in the bowl. Cover and let rise 10 more minutes. Turn out onto the board. Divide in two and shape into loaves. Place in greased loaf pans, 5x9x3-inch or 4½x8½x2¾-inch. Cover. Let rise in warm place 30 to 45 minutes or until doubled. To check, dent remains when side of dough is pressed gently with the finger. Bake 35 to 45 minutes or until well browned. Remove from pans and cool on rack. Use 400-degree preheated oven.

For 4 loaves: Double the recipe for 2 loaves, but use only 2 pkgs. yeast.
For 6 loaves: Use 3 times the recipe above, but use only 3 pkgs. yeast.
For 8 loaves: Use 4 times the recipe above, but use only 4 pkgs. yeast.
Note: In making 6 & 8 loaves, the rising times will be about 1½ times as long as those for 2 loaves.

We thank the
following people for their
time, patience and skill:

Shirley Crowell
Bob Greene
Leonard Hyams
Joanne Jablow
John Russo
George Nicolini
Bill Fisher
Carol Peretz
Bobbi Sisk
Charles Prior
Andrea Idone
David Levy

We also thank those
who contributed breads
which we were unable
to include here